HORSE

Katie Dicker

FRANKLIN WATTS
LONDON • SYDNEY

An Appleseed Editions book

Franklin Watts
First published in Great Britain in 2017
by The Watts Publishing Group

© 2013 Appleseed Editions

Created by Appleseed Editions Ltd,
Well House, Friars Hill, Guestling,
East Sussex TN35 4ET

Designed by Hel James
Edited by Mary-Jane Wilkins

ISBN hardback 978 1 4451 5105 2
Dewey Classification 636.1

A CIP catalogue for this book is available from the British Library

Photo acknowledgements
l = left, r = right, t = top, b = bottom
title iStockphoto; page 3 Lenkadan/Shutterstock; 4 Thinkstock; 5 Anastasija Popova/
Shutterstock, 6 oknoart/Shutterstock; 7 iStockphoto; 8 mariait/Shutterstock;
9 & 10 Hemera/Thinkstock; 11l Anastasija Popova/Shutterstock, r iStockphoto;
12 Wendy Kaveney Photography/Shutterstock, 13 iStockphoto; 14 Anastasija Popova/
Shutterstock; 15 Michael Cummings/Shutterstock; 16 iStockphoto, 17t vladislav_studio/
Shutterstock; 18 Graham@theGraphicZone/Shutterstock; 19t Comstock/Thinkstock,
b Thinkstock; 20l Laila Kazakevica/Shutterstock, r iStockphoto; 21lZuzule/Shutterstock,
tr bepsy/Shutterstock, br E.Spek/Shutterstock, 22 Design Pics/Thinkstock,
23 Lenkadan/Shutterstock
Cover Julia Remezova/Shutterstock

Printed in China

MIX
Paper from
responsible sources
FSC® C104740

Franklin Watts
An imprint of Hachette Children's Group
Part of The Watts Publishing Group
Carmelite House
50 Victoria Embankment
London EC4Y 0DZ

An Hachette UK Company
www.hachette.co.uk

www.franklinwatts.co.uk

Contents

My world

I am a horse.
I live on a
farm with
other horses.

During the day, we like to exercise in the fields or paddocks.

Horses are very active animals. They can walk, trot, canter and gallop.

Changing seasons

We like wide, open spaces. But we need shelter from the sun, wind and rain.

Horses can sleep standing up, but some prefer to lie down.

Zzzzz...

In winter, our stable is warm and dry. Straw and wood shavings keep us comfortable.

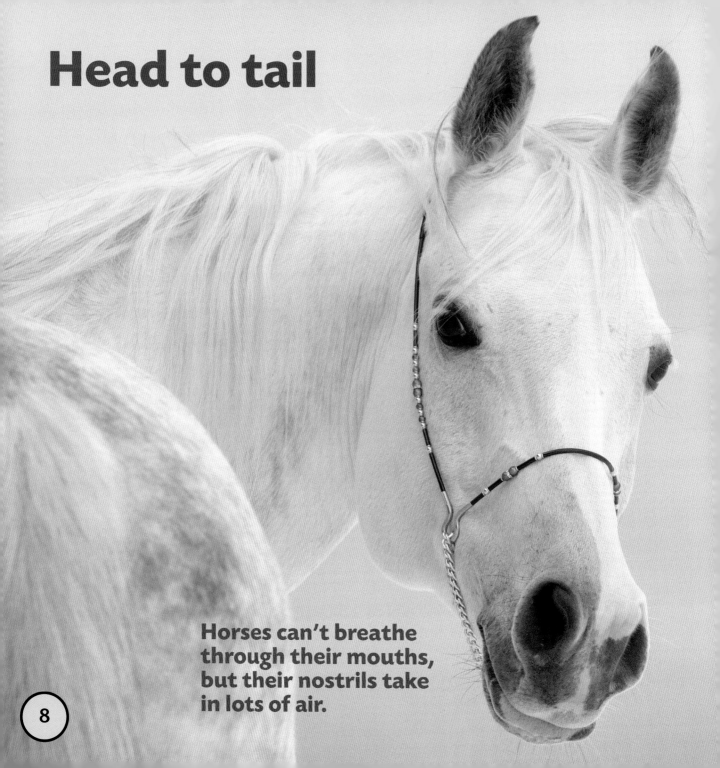

Head to tail

Horses can't breathe through their mouths, but their nostrils take in lots of air.

We have large eyes and ears to help us look and listen for danger. We use our big nostrils to breathe.

A long tail lets us swipe at itchy insects. It keeps us warm in winter too.

Most horses have a coat of grey, black or chestnut hair.

Swishhh!

Horse care

Metal shoes protect our hoofs from hard surfaces. A farrier cleans and trims our hoofs, and replaces our shoes.

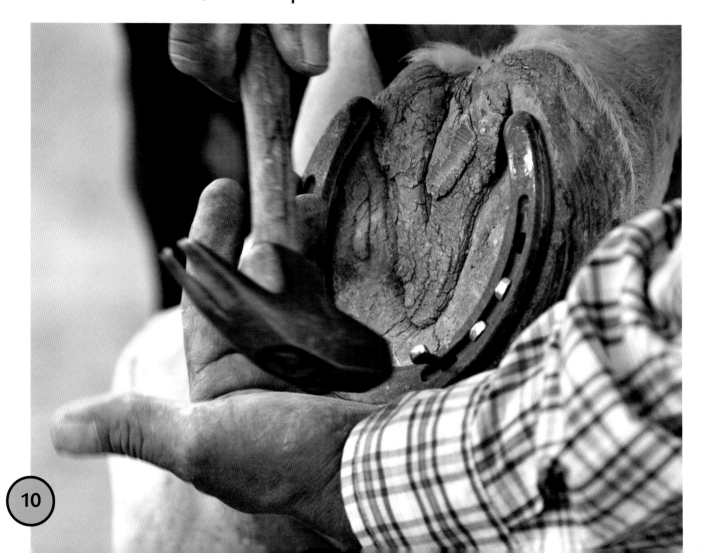

The farmer grooms our coats to keep us clean. He untangles knots in our manes and tails.

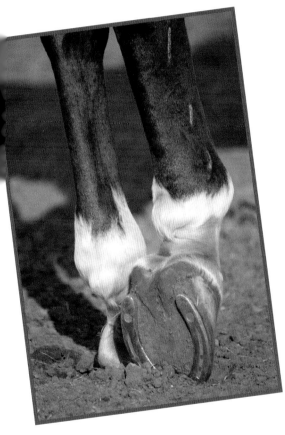

A horse's hoofs and teeth grow all through its life.

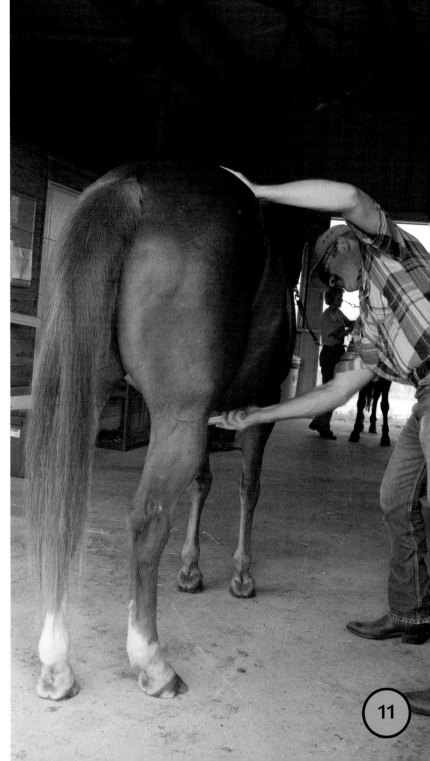

Mouth matters

Our teeth are checked regularly to keep them healthy. We need strong, even teeth to bite and chew our food.

You can tell how old a horse is by how worn its teeth are.

Our strong lips are very sensitive. They help to gather our food when we graze.

Time to eat

Our favourite foods are grass, leaves, grain and hay.

Horses also like fruits and roots, such as apples and carrots.

We drink up to 45 litres of water a day.

Mares and foals

Female horses
have baby foals
in the spring
when the weather
is warm and
there is lots
of grass to eat.

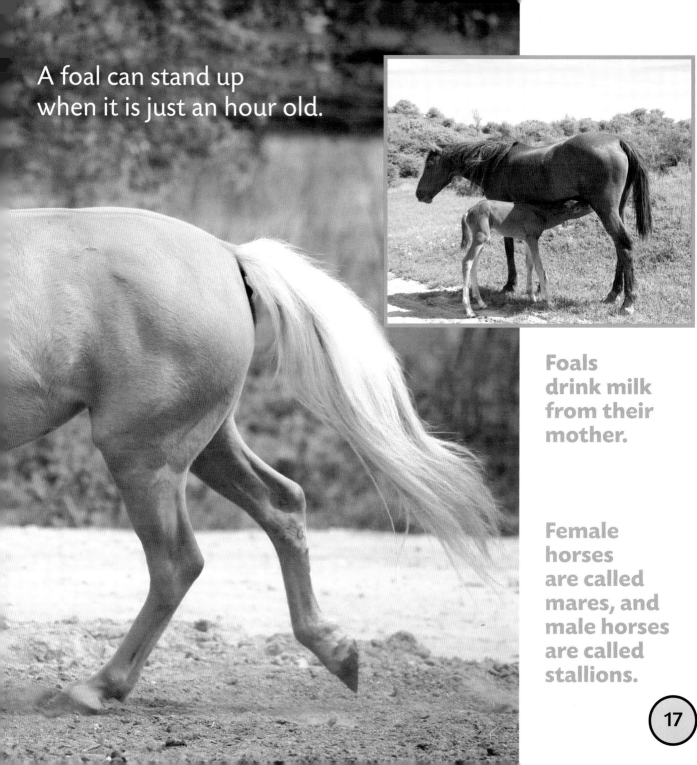

A foal can stand up when it is just an hour old.

Foals drink milk from their mother.

Female horses are called mares, and male horses are called stallions.

What horses do

In the past, farmers used horses to do heavy work on farms, such as ploughing. Most farmers now use tractors for these jobs.

Today, horses help to move animals around farms and ranches. Some people also ride horses for sport and leisure.

Horses around the world

Farmers in countries all over the world keep horses, and many horses also live in the wild. Here are some of the different breeds.

Arabian, Middle East

Appaloosa, USA

There are more than 150 different types of horses around the world.

Camargue, France

Shire, England

Shetland, Scotland

21

Did you know?

Horses use their ears to listen and to show how they feel. When a horse puts its ears back, it may be feeling angry. When it puts its ears forward, it may be feeling friendly.

Horses like company. They like to live with other horses and become loyal friends with their owners too.

Horses live for about 25 to 30 years.

Useful words

farrier
Someone who looks after horses' hoofs and fits their shoes.

gallop
A horse gallops when all four feet leave the ground with each stride.

graze
Animals graze when they eat grass in a field or pasture.

paddocks
Small fenced fields.

Index

Websites

www.animalcorner.co.uk/farm/horses/horse_about.html
www.buzzle.com/articles/horse-facts-interesting-facts-about-horses.html
http://www.activityvillage.co.uk/horses
www.ncagr.gov/cyber/kidswrld/general/barnyard/horses.htm
www.buzzle.com/articles/horse-facts-interesting-facts-about-horses.html